# CONTENTS

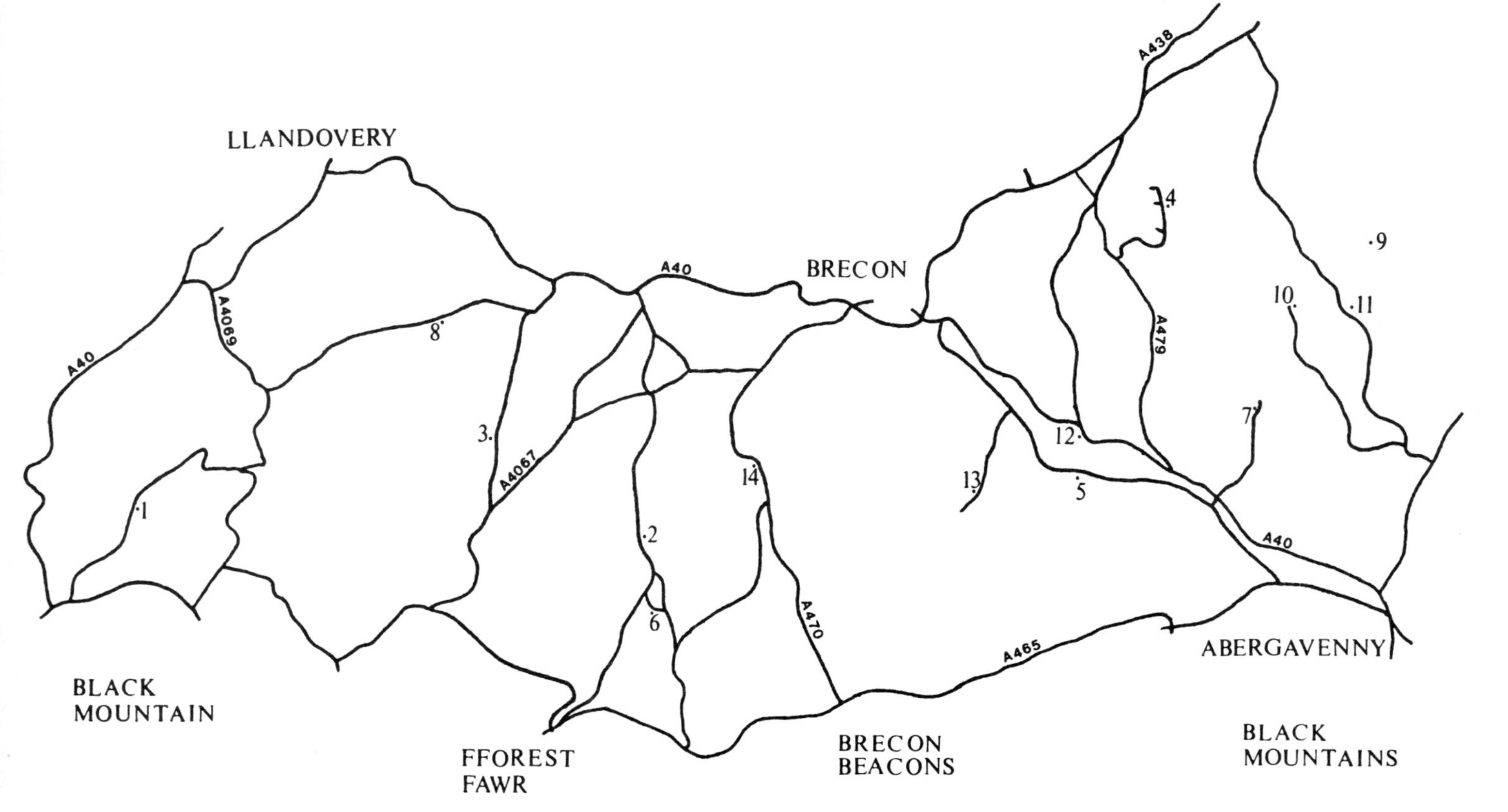
LLANDOVERY
BRECON
BLACK MOUNTAIN
FFOREST FAWR
BRECON BEACONS
ABERGAVENNY
BLACK MOUNTAINS
A40
A4069
A4067
A470
A465
A479
A438
1
2
3
4
5
6
7
8
9
10
11
12
13
14

# PUB WALKS IN THE BRECON BEACONS NATIONAL PARK

The Brecon Beacons National Park covers an area of 1344 square kilometres (519 square miles) to the north of the Welsh coal mining valleys. It is separated into four areas: from west to east, the Black Mountain, Fforest Fawr, Brecon Beacons and the Black Mountains. The routes in this guide cover all these areas but the majority are concentrated in the more popular eastern half. The fourteen walks all have a pub in the middle to provide refreshment: they are all country pubs and accustomed to walkers. All the pubs mentioned provide food of varying types, including the standard deep fried chicken or scampi with chips; often there are vegetarian alternatives. All pubs seem to be making some effort on the real ale front and the better ones are pointed out in the text. The Star Inn in Talybont gives by far the best choice of ales adding up to 150 different types over the year. The routes are put in order of difficulty and range from 8km (5 miles) to 21km (13 miles). Associated with most of the routes is an alternative route that often cuts out the mountain section and makes a pleasant walk if one is feeling lazy, not used to walking or there is just a lack of time.

Remember that the weather can change rapidly in these mountains: the temperature at the tops can be up to 6°c colder than in the valleys. The rainfall is greater and the wind can often increase at an alarming rate when one moves higher. It is often advisable to carry some extra warm and waterproof clothing and make sure that you wear stout boots for the mountains where the paths are normally rough. A map and compass are always a good idea; they can be used to identify landmarks and areas around you as well as provide assistance to navigation if you should miss the route or if the weather should deteriorate.

The location of most paths should pose no problems; most are now marked with arrows and signs, especially in the more popular areas. Remember to always stay on the paths through farmland and always close gates behind you. If in doubt of a right of way then ask, most local people are friendly and willing to assist. Most of the routes start from a suitable parking area but in some cases there is limited parking and common sense should be used when problems arise.

The most useful maps for walking the mountains and forests of the Park are the three O/S 1/25,000 Outdoor Leisure maps that cover almost the whole area; numbers 11, 12 & 13. For general touring combined with short excursions to the countryside, the 1/50,000 scale maps are adequate; sheets 160 & 161 cover most of the area except the western edge which is on 159. A free leaflet found at the Mountain Centre opens out into a very informative map that shows all the main points of interest and is well worth obtaining.

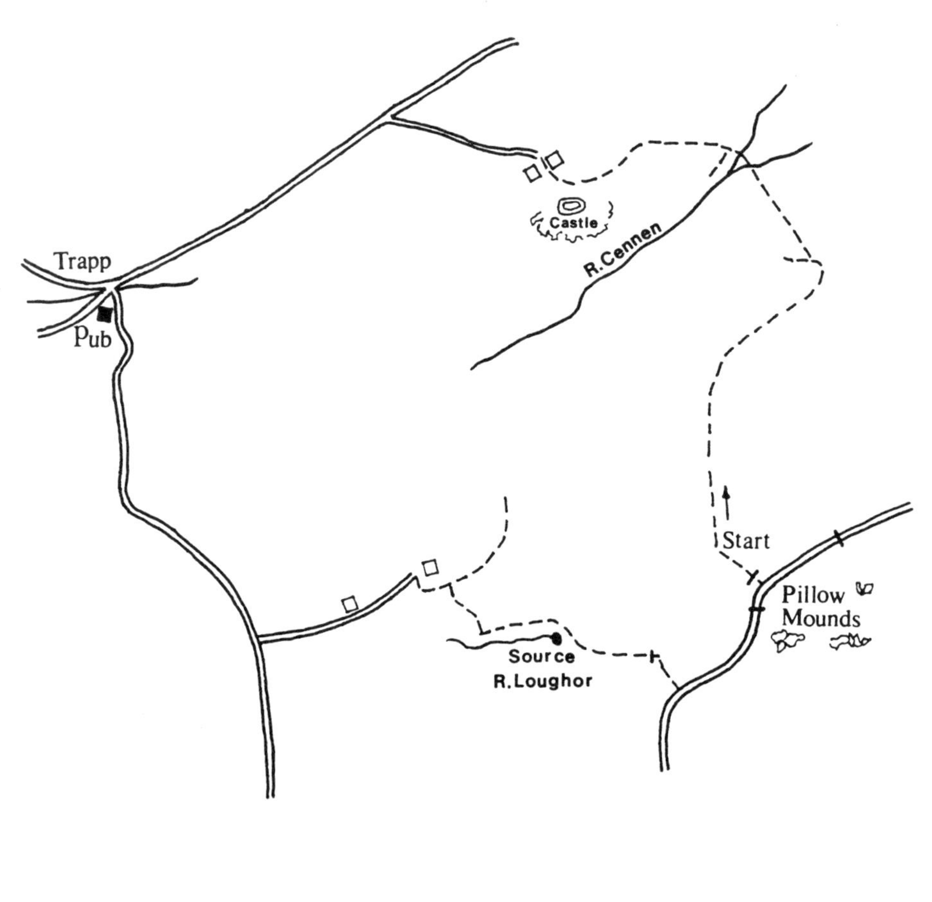
Trapp
Pub
Castle
R.Cennen
Start
Pillow
Mounds
Source
R.Loughor
0
1
2
Km

# ROUTE 1

## Carreg Cennen Castle and Trapp

**Distance:** 8km (5 miles)
**Walking Time There:** 1¼ hours
**Back:** 1 hour
**Terrain:** Easy going paths through farmland
**Paths:** Well marked out and maintained

This route is quite short and easy going. The area of the Pillow Mounds is at the western edge of the Black Mountain and looks rugged with exposed limestone boulders and outcrops all about. Carreg Cennen Castle can be seen below standing majestically on its steep and exposed limestone crag. An unusual feature of this castle is the enclosed flight of steps that have been cut into the cliffs to a cave below. The purpose of this cave is unsure but you can visit it with a torch and decide for yourself if the possibilities of a dovecot or defensive structure are correct. The castle has had a long and troubled history; its date of building is unknown but it was finally put out of action by being demolished by a gang of 500 workmen in 1462 to stop the Welsh from using it. The village of Trapp is small and well kept – in fact a sign announces as you enter that it is 'The Best Kept Village in Dyfed'. The Cennen Arms is well situated near the river Cennen and is popular all year round. Very good food and a range of ales are served in the well laid out and pleasing interior. On the way back from the pub you will pass the source of the river Loughor which issues forth from underground through a large crack in the limestone. It is the collapse of this limestone into underground watercourses that causes the many shake holes that are common in this area.

1. Start at the western end of the Pillow Mounds on the road overlooking Carreg Cennen Castle, **SN674180.**

*Carreg Cennen Castle on its limestone crag.*

*Carreg Cennen Castle from the Pillow Mounds.*

2. Go through a gate and onto the track following the castle symbol signpost. The track is not far from the 'private' cattle grid at the western end of the Pillow Mounds.
3. Carry on downhill and follow the white or yellow footpath markers. After going around a tight left hand bend go over a stile with steps on the other side. This track is again marked by a castle symbol.
4. After crossing two wooden bridges take the footpath that goes uphill to the castle.
5. After looking at the castle follow the track in the direction marked Castell Farm.
6. Walk through the farm and past its associated gift shop and tea-shop. Follow the road beyond the farm.
7. Walk on this road to a junction and turn left. Continue downhill into the village of Trapp and the welcome sight of the Cennen Arms.
8. Come out of the pub and turn right along the road. Walk uphill along this road for 1km and turn left over a cattle grid and onto a track signposted for Heol y Cwrt.
9. Walk up to the farmhouse and follow the yellow arrows around to the right and along another track.
10. Turn right onto another track signposted with the castle symbol and a yellow arrow.
11. On the right hand side about 500m along the track can be found the source of the river Loughor. Another 300m and the track comes to an open field. Go right at this field and onto the road via a stile.
12. Turn left at the road and walk back to the start point.

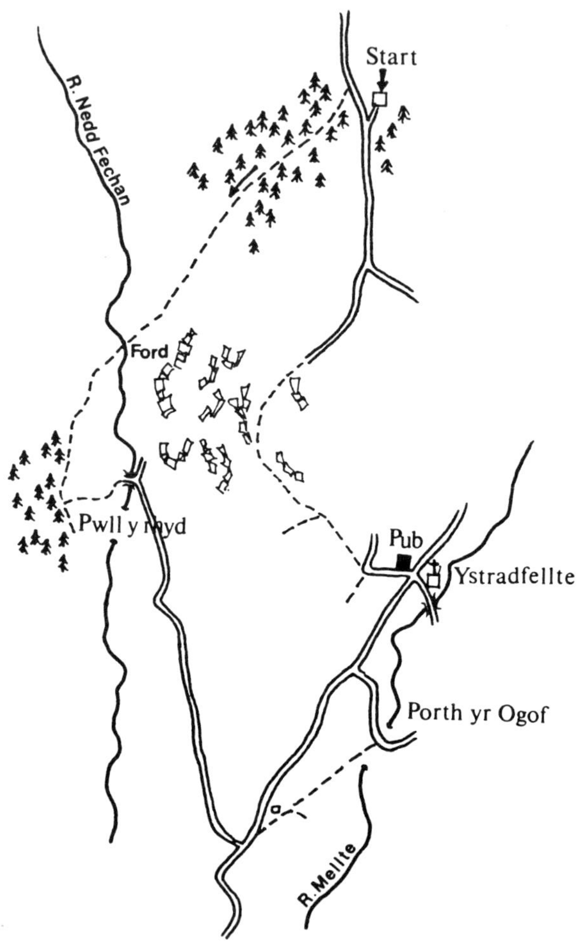
Start
R. Nedd Fechan
Ford
Pwll y rhyd
Pub
Ystradfellte
Porth yr Ogof
R. Mellte

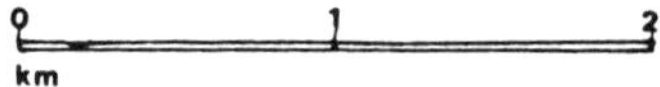
0
1
2
km

# ROUTE 2

## Roman Road and Disappearing River

**Distance:** 13km (8 miles)
**Walking Time There:** $2^1/_2$ hours
**Back:** 1 hour
**Terrain:** Easy going but a river needs to be forded
**Paths:** Well marked and easy to follow

This is an easy walk except for the crossing of the Nedd Fechan which could prove problematic if the river is too high – you can always take off your boots to cross if the weather is warm. The detour to Pwll y Rhyd is fascinating because the river can be seen to disappear into a deep hole in the limestone rock. If the river has already dried up then it is possible to get down to the large caves that lie on either side of the pool at the bottom. The river can be found again by walking further downstream through a mini gorge, overgrown with plants and trees, to a cave from which it reappears. Further along the route will be found the popular attraction of Porth yr Ogof, which is a large cave mouth into which the river Mellte disappears. If the water level is low it is possible to enter the cave and sometimes see the white deposits on a back wall. These deposits are said to look like a horse and thus the name White Horse Cave is often used. The New Inn at Ystradfellte caters for most needs (see also route 14). The walk back goes through the area of limestone crags known as Carnau Gwynion from where it is possible to see the mountains of Fforest Fawr rising in the north.

1. Start at the Forestry Commission carpark and picnic site at SN927165.
2. Walk from the carpark back to the road – turn right, walk for 200m and turn left, go through a gate and along a bridleway through a plantation.
3. Follow the track, which is actually a Roman road, out of the plantation, past Maen Madoc standing stone and down to the river Nedd Fechan (Neath). Cross the river at a suitable point.
4. Continue to follow the track on the other side of the river. Come to a junction at the top of the track – turn left following the wooden signpost that reads Sarn Helen.
5. After 500m there is a slight left hand bend in the track and a gate – just after this turn left down another track. There are shake holes at the side of this junction. Follow this track until you again reach the river.
6. Cross the river via a bridge and gate to the small car parking area. It is now time to take a short detour to the strange area around Pwll y Rhyd. To the right of the gate there is a stile which leads to the river bank, which can then be followed for 200m to Pwll y Rhyd.

*Maen Madoc at the side of the Sarn Helen Roman road.*

7. Go around Pwll y Rhyd and over a stile to follow an old river course. Be careful as it is often very slippery.
8. Retrace your steps back to the bridge and carpark (6).
9. Follow the dirt road that leads from the carpark up a steep slope to a junction. Turn right onto a narrow open road.
10. After $2^1/_2$km another road is met. Turn left and then, after a short distance, right through a gate and onto a track marked for Porth yr Ogof.
11. Follow the track for 250m and then turn left onto a path signposted with blue arrows. This path can be followed to the carpark above the great cave entrance of Porth yr Ogof which can be found by following the nearby signposts.
12. After visiting Porth yr Ogof come back to the carpark. Turn right out of the carpark and follow the road uphill to a junction – turn right at the junction and follow the road downhill to the New Inn and the village of Ystradfellte.
13. Upon leaving the pub turn right and follow the narrow lane past the carpark.
14. After 300m the lane bends right towards Tyle Farm – take the track that is directly in front of you. Go through two gates and continue to follow the track between the crags to another gate. Go through this gate onto a track bounded by limestone walls.
15. Turn left when the track meets a road and follow it back to the starting point at the Forestry Commission carpark.

**Alternative Route:**
See the alternative on route 14 that starts at the same carpark.

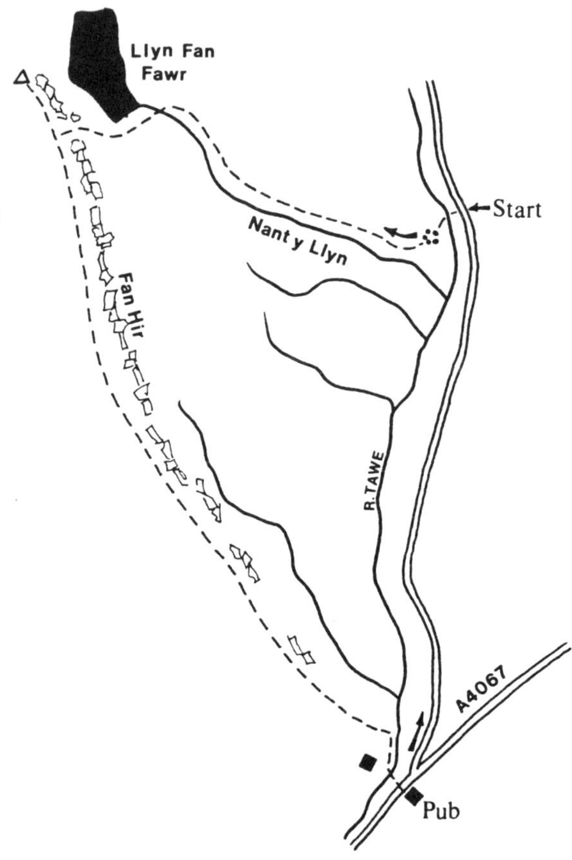
Llyn Fan
Fawr
Start
Nant y Llyn
Fan Hir
R.TAWE
A4067
Pub

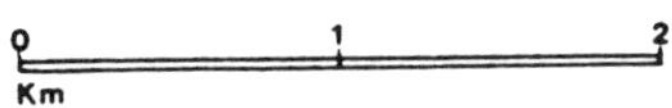
0
1
2
Km

# ROUTE 3

## Mountain Lake and Tafarn y Garreg

**Distance:** 11km (7miles)
**Walking Time There:** $2^1/_2$ hours
**Back:** 1 hour
**Terrain:** Open moorland – some very steep ascents
**Paths:** Small and indistinct on the mountains

This route is perfect for a warm summers day and combines the attractions of a mountain stream, lake and a high ridge with extensive views; this is followed by a welcome stop at a charming inn and a pleasant walk back. Cerrig Duon at the start of the route is a circle of low stones accompanied by a larger one called Maen Mawr: they are thought to be of Bronze Age origin and their position and possible use is certainly thought provoking, though opinion is always divided on their purpose. The approach to Llyn y Fan Fawr is deceptive as the view to it is initially blocked by the large terminal moraine that caused its formation nearly 10,000 years ago at the end of the Great Ice Age. The lake is overshadowed by the cliffs of Fan Brycheiniog and

*Llyn y Fan Fawr from Fan Brycheiniog.*

has a quality of isolation and serenity that is only just matched by its neighbour, Llyn y Fan Fach, on the other side of the mountain. The view from the ridge of Fan Hir is extensive in all directions – at its base can be seen a good example of a lateral moraine formed by a mass of ice pushing debris in front of it: when the glacier melted it left the great mounds of rocks and earth to remind us of its awesome power. The Tafarn y Garreg is a traditional inn that has three bars, one with settles, and a cosy dining area. The walk back is along a country lane and is a welcome change after the open mountains. The road from which to start from can be reached by following the signs for Dan yr Ogof caves on the A4067 – shortly after the entrance to the showcave complex you

*A waterfall on Nant y Llyn.*

should turn left onto a country lane signposted for Trecastle. The stone circle of Cerrig Duon lies to the left hand side of the road on the top of a small rise halfway up the valley – it is difficult to spot from the road.

1. Start at the stone circle of Cerrig Duon at SN852207, which is close to various small parking areas at the side of the road in the upper Tawe valley.
2. Walk south, back down the valley, for about 250m from Cerrig Duon and turn right onto a faint path at the side of the deeply eroded course of Nant y Llyn. This path can be followed along the side of the stream, past numerous waterfalls, until it reaches the lake of Llyn y Fan Fawr. The stream disappears just in front of some mounds – walk over the mounds in the direction of the cliffs beyond to find the lake.
3. Follow the narrow rocky path to the left of the lake up the great cliffs of Fan Brycheiniog until you reach the top of the cwm.
4. At the top of the cwm do not follow the path as it bends to the right, but turn left and walk along the top of the ridge called Fan Hir.
5. Follow the faint track across Fan Hir and descend into the valley at the end.
6. The track becomes very indistinct and bends to the right as you descend. Head for the gate at the left hand side of the sheepfold near the house below.
7. Go over the gate and follow the yellow arrows. Turn right at the river and walk to a footbridge. Go over the footbridge and walk the short distance to the road and the Tafarn y Garreg Inn.
8. Upon leaving the inn cross the road and turn right. Shortly after turn left onto the country lane to Trecastle. Follow this lane back up the valley to the stone circle and the starting point.

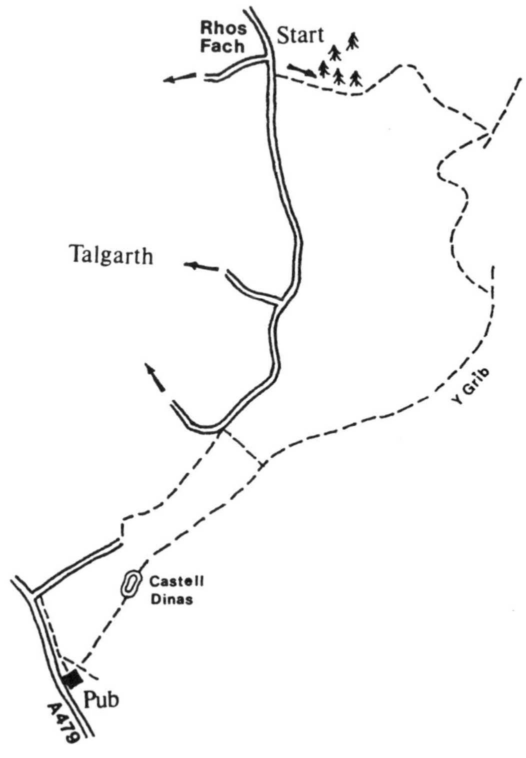
Rhos
Fach
Start
Talgarth
Y Grib
Castell
Dinas
Pub
A479

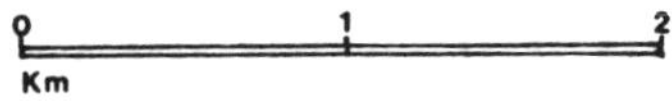
0
1
2
Km

# ROUTE 4

## Black Mountains and Castell Dinas

**Distance:** 11km (7miles)
**Walking Time There:** 2 hours
**Back:** 1 hour
**Terrain:** Open mountain followed by tracks and road
**Paths:** Easy to follow

This walk starts with a very steep ascent up the northern escarpments of the Black Mountains. Once at the top the walker is rewarded with extensive views across the Wye valley and the mountains of Mid Wales. Castell Dinas is what remains of an Iron Age hillfort or defended farmstead: the remains of the various ramparts can still be clearly seen. Inside the hillfort there are the ruins of a Norman castle – but there is very little left to see. The Castle Inn at Pengenffordd serves real ale and is popular with the pony-trekkers of the area: there is a 'Trekers Barn' provided next to the main pub especially for walkers and equestrians. The main pub has an open fire that goes well with the friendly atmosphere and comfortable surroundings. It is recommended in the 1992 Good Beer Guide. The walk back is easy and provides a different view of the steep escarpments and farmland of the Black Mountains. It is possible to park cars along the verge at Rhos Fach, which can be found by following the roads from Talgarth on the A479.

*Castell Dinas from the ridge of Y Grib.*

*The remains of the Norman castle at Castell Dinas.*

1. Start at Rhos Fach, SO188334.
2. Take the wide track that leads east towards the escarpment of the Black Mountains. The track has 'no entry' signs for vehicles and a pine forest on its left side.
3. Keep following the track up the steep ascent of Rhiw Cwmstab to the rocky top.
4. On reaching the top turn right along a narrow path and follow it along the top of the escarpment.
5. Follow the path around the head of a valley but do not descend into it.
6. Continue across the open mountain and around the head of the next valley. In front of you is the ridge of Y Grib dropping down to the right and ending at Castell Dinas. The steep sides of Mynydd Troed can be seen across the valley.
7. Continue to follow the path along the ridge of Y Grib until you reach the open area below Castell Dinas.
8. Go over the stile provided and walk to the top of Castell Dinas.
9. Cross the top and walk down the opposite side and follow a path to the right. White arrows guide you down to a stile.
10. Continue to follow the path marked by white arrows until a track is reached. Turn right and after a short distance you will join the main road.
11. Turn left at the road and The Castle Inn is about 100m on the left.
12. Turn right out of the pub and walk to a track that runs parallel to the road but is separated by a hedge. Follow this track to a narrow lane.
13. Turn right up the lane and follow it around the base of the castell until a public footpath sign is reached on the right.
14. Follow the footpath to the open area below Castell Dinas – turn left to follow a track that runs below Y Grib.
15. After 800m the track joins the right angle bend of a road. Turn right at this road and follow it for 2½km back to Rhos Fach.

**Alternative Route:** 4½km (3 miles)
Start at the right hand bend of the road mentioned in instruction 15, SO185312. Ascend the steep side of Y Grib and turn right along the top of the ridge. Follow the main route from instruction 7.

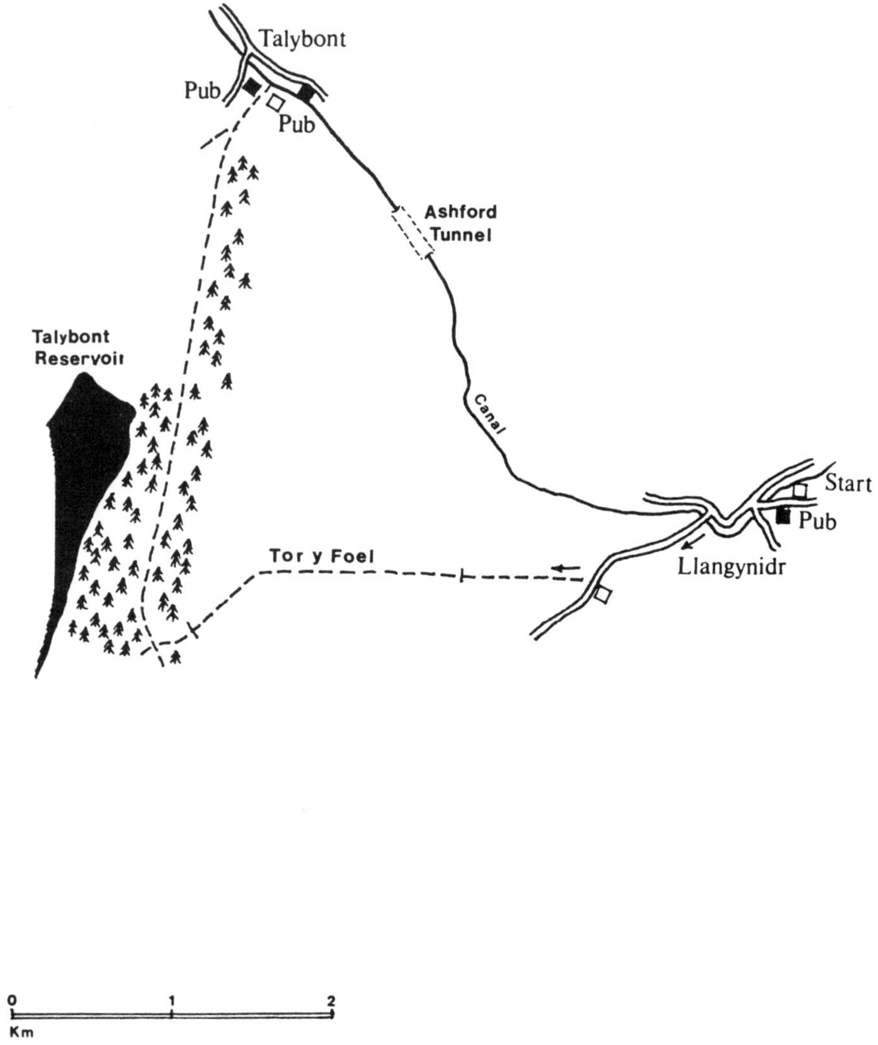

Talybont
Pub
Pub
Ashford
Tunnel
Talybont
Reservoir
Canal
Start
Pub
Llangynidr
Tor y Foel
0
1
2
Km

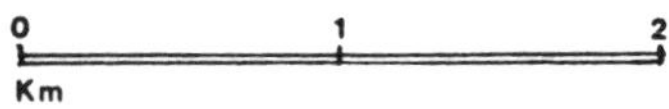

# ROUTE 5

## Talybont and the Canal Towpath

**Distance:** 13km (8 miles)
**Walking Time There:** $2^1/_2$ hours
**Back:** $1^1/_2$ hours
**Terrain:** Roads, tracks and canal towpath
**Paths:** Well marked and easy to follow

The walk from Llangynidr to Tor y Foel is quite arduous but after this initial section the rest of the walk is easy going. The summit of Tor y Foel is rather deceptive because it rises in steps; the top of each step seems like the final summit until you cross it and find another ascent in front of you. The forest track provides a nice contrast from the open mountain. Along the track can be seen the stones used for the railway that once past this way. The village of Talybont is very popular and can become crowded at the height of the season. There are three pubs within a short walk of each other – the White Hart Inn, the Star Inn and the Travellers Rest. The White Hart Inn and the Star Inn are both suitable for walkers. The Star Inn was CAMRA's Mid and South Wales Pub of the Year in 1989 and serves "at least a dozen real ales, constantly varied", so there should be plenty of choice. Also provided are bar snacks and a large garden next to the river. The Travellers Rest is more upmarket with a comfortable interior. There is a warm and friendly atmosphere with log fires, real ale and a good range of homemade foods: muddy boots may not be a good idea, though there is a garden at the back that overlooks the canal. The navigable part of the canal now runs from Brecon to Pontypool and can be followed the whole way along the towpath. An interesting feature at the end of the walk is the locks near to Llangynidr. The Coach and Horses Tavern at Llangynidr is an alternative stop and provides the necessary real ales and food which can be consumed in the garden across the road overlooking the canal. It is recommended in the 1991 Good Beer Guide.

1. Start at the Coach and Horses Tavern at the west end of Llangynidr on the B4558, SO146199.
2. Turn right out of the carpark and walk round the 'U' bend of the road.
3. After the bend turn immediately left, go over the canal and onto a country road.
4. Follow this road for 1km and then, at the top of the hill, turn right onto a way-marked footpath opposite a house.
5. Continue along this footpath to the open mountain and on to the top of Tor y Foel.
6. Continue to follow the path as it turns left from the summit of Tor y Foel until you reach a rough track.
7. Cross the track and continue downhill on a narrow path to the forest edge and an old gate.

*The locks and towpath near Llangynidr.*

Go over the gate and walk down through the trees.

8. Shortly you will meet a wide forest track – turn right.
9. Follow this track straight on for 4km to the village of Talybont.
10. At the end of the track you will cross a canal bridge and immediately find the White Hart Inn. Turn left at the road and the Star Inn will be found a little way up on the left. The third pub can be found by starting on the route back along the canal – after 500m the Travellers Rest will be found on the left hand side.
11. Upon leaving either pub in Talybont walk to the canal behind the White Hart Inn and turn left onto the towpath. From the Travellers Rest walk to the rear and rejoin the towpath.
12. Continue along the towpath until you reach the Ashford Tunnel. At this point you must leave the canal and walk the 500m along the road to rejoin the towpath at the other end of the tunnel.
13. The towpath can now be followed directly back to Llangynidr.

**Alternative Route A:** 5km (3 miles)
For a pleasant walk along the canal only you can start at Llangynidr and follow the towpath to Talybont and the choice of three pubs. Return by the same route.

**Alternative Route B:** 5km (3 miles)
If you prefer to stop at the Coach and Horses Tavern in Llangynidr then start at the village of Talybont and follow the main route from instruction number 11 along the towpath. Return by the same route.

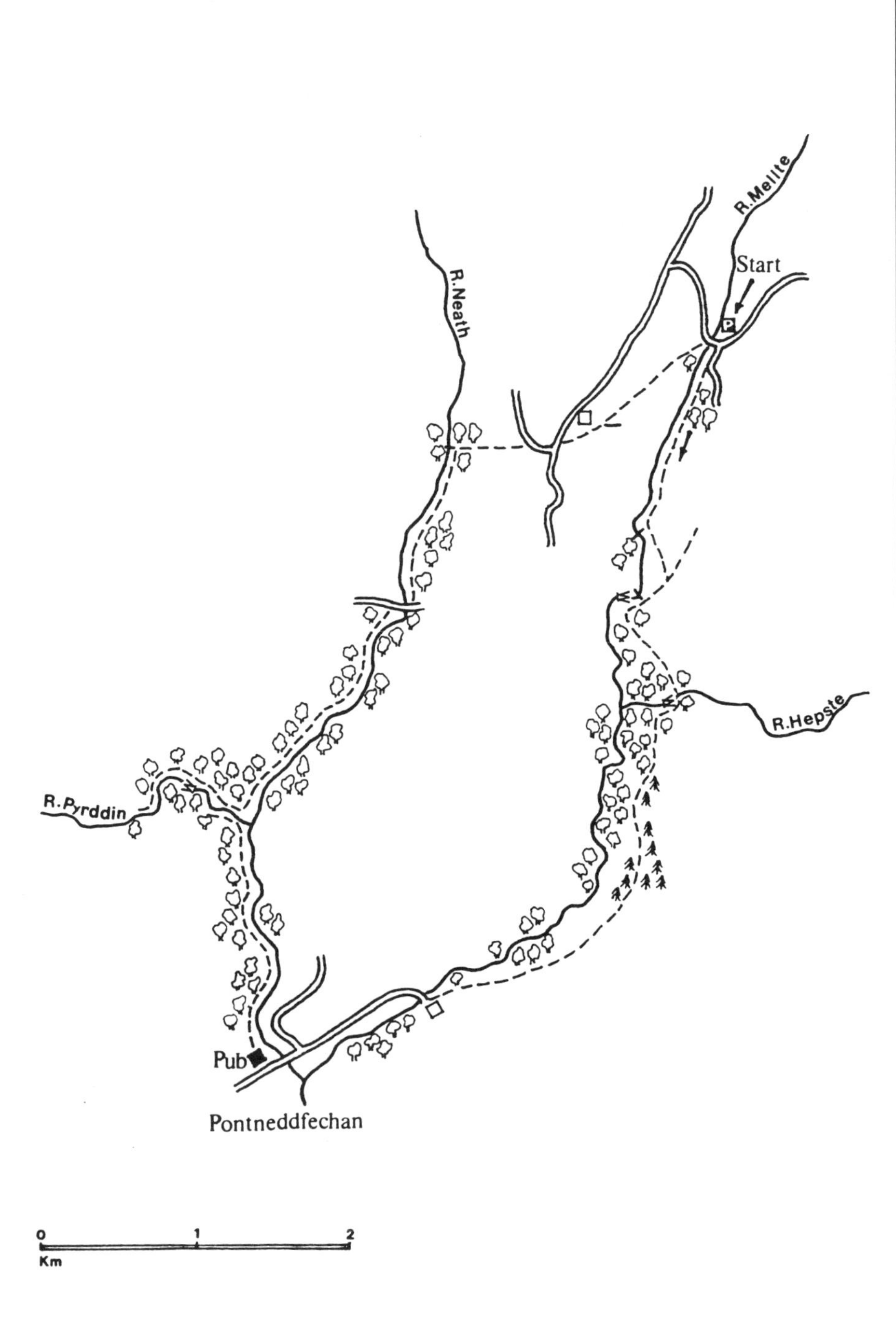

R.Mellte
Start
P
R.Neath
R.Hepste
R.Pyrddin
Pub
Pontneddfechan
0
1
2
Km

# ROUTE 6

## Rivers, Waterfalls and Pontneddfechan

**Distance:** 13km (8 miles)
**Walking Time There:** $2^1/_2$ hours
**Back:** 2 hours
**Terrain:** Woodland and riverside
**Paths:** Well marked and easy to follow

This walk covers most of what has become known as the Waterfall Country of the Brecon Beacons. Running through this area are four main rivers; the Pyrddin, Nedd Fechan (or Neath), Mellte, and Hepste: all of which can be seen on this walk. These rivers originate in the open heathland of Fforest Fawr to the north and converge at Pontneddfechan. Before the rivers reach Pontneddfechan they cross the narrow belt of Carboniferous Limestone and Millstone Grit which lies along the southern edge of the park. It is here that they carve out the varied landscape of rocky ravines, caves, deep potholes, and a variety of spectacular waterfalls – including the Hanging Waterfall (Sgwd yr Eira) behind which this route will take you. Pontneddfechan is a popular village which has a choice of venues: a hotel that does plenty of bar meals, the Old White Horse Inn, and The Angel that has a specially designed 'Hikers Bar' with tiled floor which is supplemented by seating outside. The Angel does excellent food and serves real ales in a pleasant atmosphere.

1. Start at the Porth Yr Ogof carpark, SN928124.
2. Follow the well marked footpath across the road opposite the carpark. Go over the slippery limestone boulders to meet the river Mellte.
3. Follow the course of the river downstream. After 2km see a small footbridge on your right. Do not cross the bridge but follow the way-marked path to the waterfall called Sgwd Clun-Gwyn; better known as the Upper Fall.
4. Continue to follow the course of the river downstream until you meet a sign that warns of dangerous paths. Take the path to the left of the sign and walk up above the river. (To see the other waterfalls, follow the paths close to the river for approx 1km downstream – to return to the main path, either come back to the danger sign or walk up the steep slopes to the left of the last fall).
5. Continue along the path until you reach some wooden steps to the right. Descend these steps down the steep valley side to the valley of the river Hepste.
6. At the bottom of the valley will be found the Hanging Waterfall. The river can be crossed by the path that leads behind the fall.
7. Ascend the steep slope on the opposite side of the waterfall and turn right at the top.
8. Carry on in a southerly direction across the top of Craig y Ddinas. Follow the signs for Ddinas Rock.

*The Hanging Waterfall on the river Hepste.*

9. Follow the track down to the carpark at the base of the rock. Go through the carpark and turn right across a bridge and onto the road.
10. After about 1km you arrive in Pontneddfechan where you have a choice of three pubs.
11. After the pub go through the gate marked Lady's Waterfall at the rear of The Angel pub.
12. Follow the river Neath upstream along a wide track until you reach a footbridge.
13. At the footbridge either a: go left to see Lady's Fall, or, b: cross and turn left to follow the course of the river Pyrddin for about 2km to see the Crooked Fall as well, or, c: cross the footbridge, turn right and continue to follow the river Neath. This (c) is the main route and should be rejoined after any diversions.
14. Continue to follow the river Neath to a carpark and picnic area. Walk through the carpark and cross the road and bridge – immediately after the bridge turn left over a stile signposted for Pont Rhyd-y-cnau. Take the path that is immediately to the right and continue along the course of the river Neath.
15. Upon reaching another smaller bridge turn right along the bridleway following the signs for Gwaun Bryn-bwch.
16. At the top of the bridleway go through a gate and turn right along a narrow road.
17. After a short distance turn left and then right through a gate and onto a track marked for Porth yr Ogof.
18. Follow the track for 250m and then turn left onto a path signposted with blue arrows. This path can be followed to the point where you started opposite the carpark.

**Alternative Route:** 7km (4 miles)
Start at the carpark and picnic site mentioned in instruction 15, SN908105. Follow the footpath that heads downstream along the river Neath. Upon reaching the footbridge the detours at instruction 14 can be taken to the other falls. Continue to follow the river Neath into Pontneddechan and the pubs. After the pub retrace your route following instructions 12-15 back to the carpark.

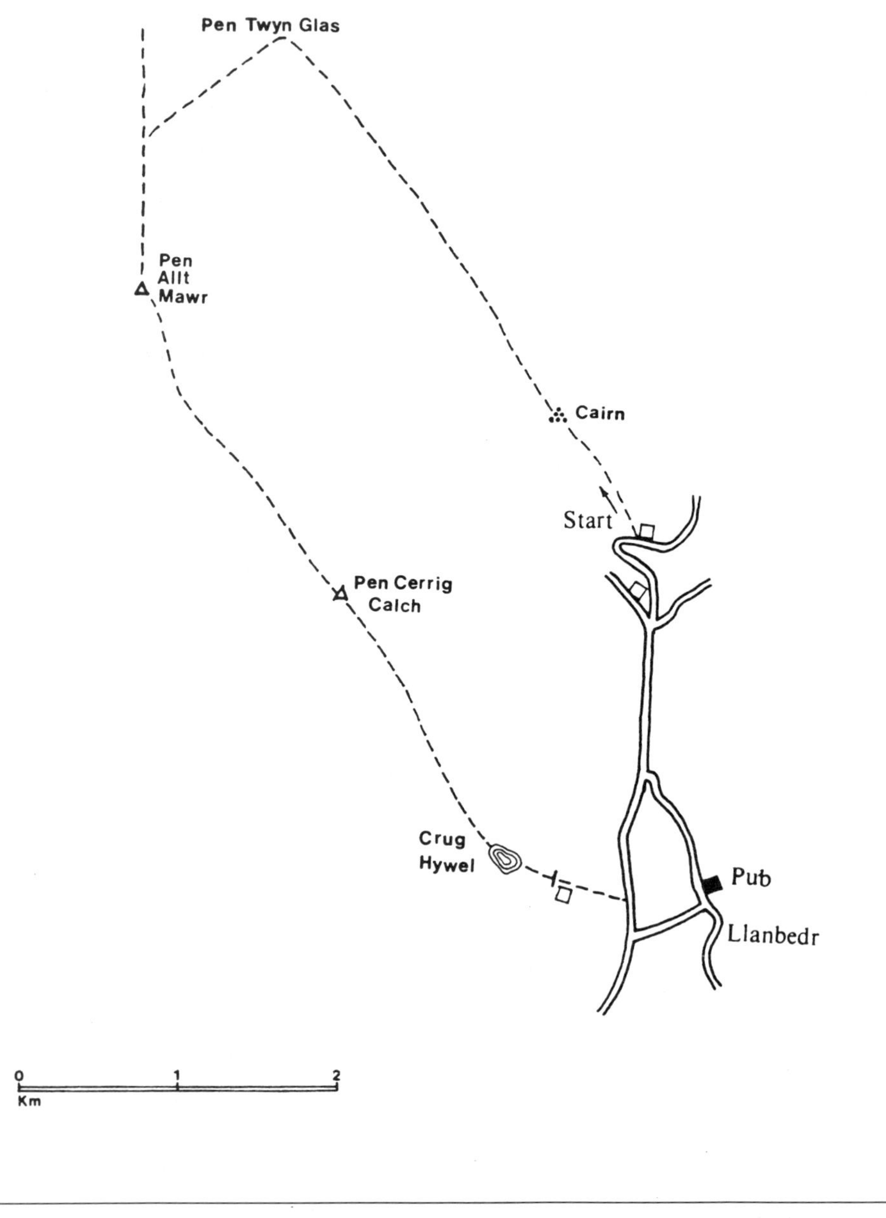
Pen Twyn Glas
Pen
Allt
Mawr
Cairn
Start
Pen Cerrig
Calch
Crug
Hywel
Pub
Llanbedr
0
1
2
Km

# ROUTE 7

## Pen Cerrig-calch and Llanbedr

**Distance:** 14km ($8^1/_2$ miles)
**Walking Time There:** $3^1/_4$ hours
**Back:** 45 min
**Terrain:** Open mountain and road – some steep ascents and descents
**Paths:** Generally good

Pen Allt-mawr and Pen Cerrig-calch are both limestone peaks in contrast to the usual Old Red Sandstone that forms the other mountains of the area. Around the sloping edges of the peaks there are piles of eroded rocks gradually moving downhill; while across the tops there are boulders of grey glistening limestone strewn across the contrasting black peat. These peaks will often have a wind blowing across them, almost gale force at times, no matter what the weather is like in the valley below: high winds are often hard to walk in but are certainly invigorating. Crug Hywel is an Iron Age hillfort and is worth a visit to see the ramparts and admire the view over the valley that the inhabitants of this great construction must have had. The walk down from Pen Cerrig-calch gives a good bird's-eye view of the forts layout. The Red Lion at Llanbedr does good food and excellent real ales. Regular guest ales are stocked and it is recommended in the 1992 Good Beer Guide. There is a cosy interior with a low ceiling, fireplace and rugs on the floor and is popular with visiting equestrians – but watch the muddy boots because the landlords a bit fussy and you may have to take them off. To get to the start point go to Crickhowell and take the road signposted for Llanbedr. Upon reaching the village drive straight through and turn right at a junction, follow this road until it drops down into a narrow valley, at the bottom go around the hairpin bend and the carpark space is on the left hand side.

1. Start at the parking area on the road from Crickhowell to the Grwyne Fechan valley, SO235228.
2. Go over a stile at the side of the carpark and follow the white arrows and signs that read 'To The Mountain'.
3. Continue to the open mountain, past small disused quarry pits, to a cairn. Turn right at this cairn and continue along the ridge to the top of Pen Twyn Glas. As you ascend this ridge the peaks of Pen Allt-mawr and Pen Cerrig-calch can be seen rising to your left.
4. Upon reaching the top of Pen Twyn Glas turn left along another narrow path and the steep ascent to the rocky summit of Pen Allt-mawr.
5. Follow the path from the summit across the saddle that separates Pen Allt-mawr and Pen Cerrig-calch until you come to another trig' point.
6. From here you can walk downhill to the hillfort of Crug Hywel, also known as Table Mountain.

*The view from below Pen Allt-mawr.*

7. Follow the path that heads downhill to the left of Crug Hywel. After 100m leave the path and cut downhill towards two buildings.
8. Go through a gate and then continue downhill to a gate at the side of the two buildings. Turn left after this gate and follow the track downhill.
9. At the bottom of the hill the track meets a road – turn right and walk along the road for 500m.
10. Turn left onto another road and into the village of Llanbedr where you will find The Red Lion.
11. Turn right out of the pub and follow the narrow lane out of the village.
12. After 1km come to a junction and turn right.
13. After another 1km come to a white cottage with three lanes heading off – continue straight on along the middle lane to the right of the cottage.
14. Follow this road for 600m back to the carpark.

**Alternative Route:** $4^1/_2$km (3 miles)
Follow the main instructions for reaching the parking area, but after approx $1^1/_2$km (1 mile) out of Llanbedr there is an area of restricted parking on the left near a cottage. The footpath is signposted to the side of the cottage. Upon meeting the open mountain continue uphill for a little way and turn left upon meeting another footpath. Follow this path to the hillfort of Crug Hywel. After the hillfort follow the main route from instruction number 7 to the pub and back along the road to your parking area.

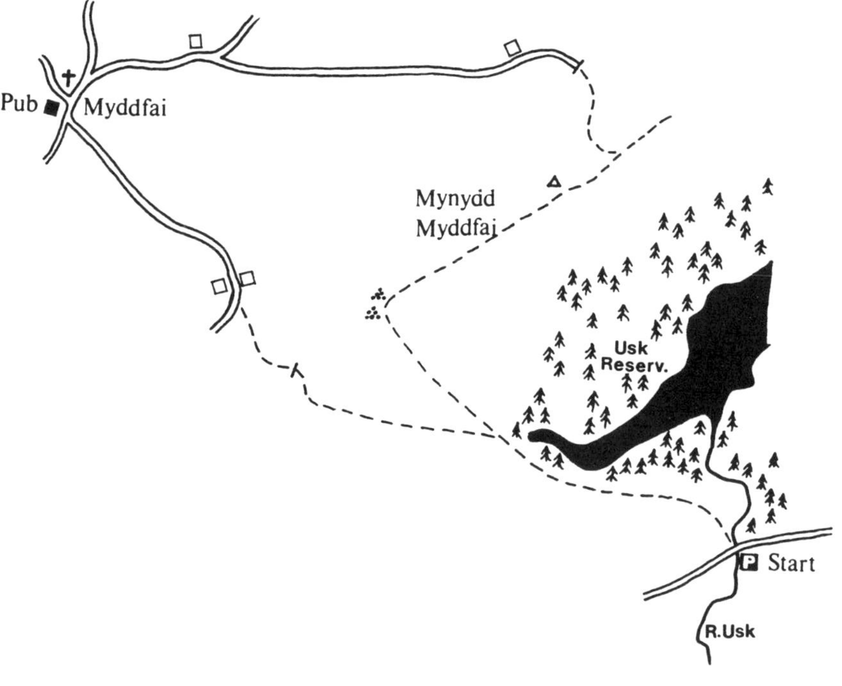
Pub
Myddfai
Mynydd
Myddfai
Usk
Reserv.
Start
R.Usk
0
1
2
Km

# ROUTE 8

## Mountain and village of Myddfai

**Distance:** 15km (9 miles)
**Walking Time There:** 2 hours
**Back:** $1^1/_2$ hours
**Terrain:** Open mountain and farmland
**Paths:** Very few across the mountain but obvious in the valley

This walk starts at the Forestry Commission carpark below the Black Mountain and can be reached by following the signs to the Usk reservoir from Trecastle – this carpark is towards the western end of the reservoir. The initial part of this walk is across open country and should not be attempted in bad weather unless you are properly equipped. There is a good all round view from Mynydd Myddfai which takes in the reservoir below, the north ridges of the Black Mountain and the lowland valleys to the north and west of the Park. The open mountain is followed by a walk through peaceful farmland and then into the pleasant and well kept village of Myddfai with its neat cottages and church. Here you will find the Plough Inn that serves good food and real ale in a friendly atmosphere. The village is known from the tale of the Physicians of Myddfai, whose mother came from the lake of Llyn y Fan Fach that nestles below the ridge of Bannau Sir Gaer in the Black Mountain.

*The river Usk near the reservoir.*

1. Start at the Forestry Commission carpark at Pont'ar Wysg, SN820271.
2. Cross the cattle grid outside the forest carpark and turn right onto the open mountain.

*The open country around the Usk reservoir.*

3. Head across the open ground to the corner of the forestry plantation that surrounds the Usk reservoir on your right.
4. Turn left along the course of an old bank and ditch and continue around the plantation until you reach a small but wide bottomed valley at the end of the reservoir.
5. Cross the valley and head up to the top of the hill directly in front – at the left hand end of Mynydd Myddfai – you will see some low cairns.
6. At the top turn right and continue along the ridge to the trig' point at the top of Mynydd Myddfai – about $1^1/_2$km.
7. Continue past the trig' point in the same direction. After a short distance meet a track and turn left along it.
8. Follow the track downhill until it reaches a gate. Go through the gate and follow the narrow road along the valley.
9. After $2^1/_2$km come to a junction with a road – turn left and follow the road for 1km into the village of Myddfai and The Plough Inn.
10. Turn right out of the pub, walk past some cottages and then take the first left.
11. Walk up this road for $1^1/_2$km, pass between two buildings and then immediately follow the bridleway directly in front of you marked with a blue arrow.
12. The bridleway should be followed straight ahead, do not follow the blue arrow to the left just after the gate. Continue up the bridleway until the open mountain is reached.
13. Take the right hand path after the gate to the open mountain. Follow this path around the hill until the reservoir comes into view.
14. From here you can retrace your steps back around the end of the reservoir.

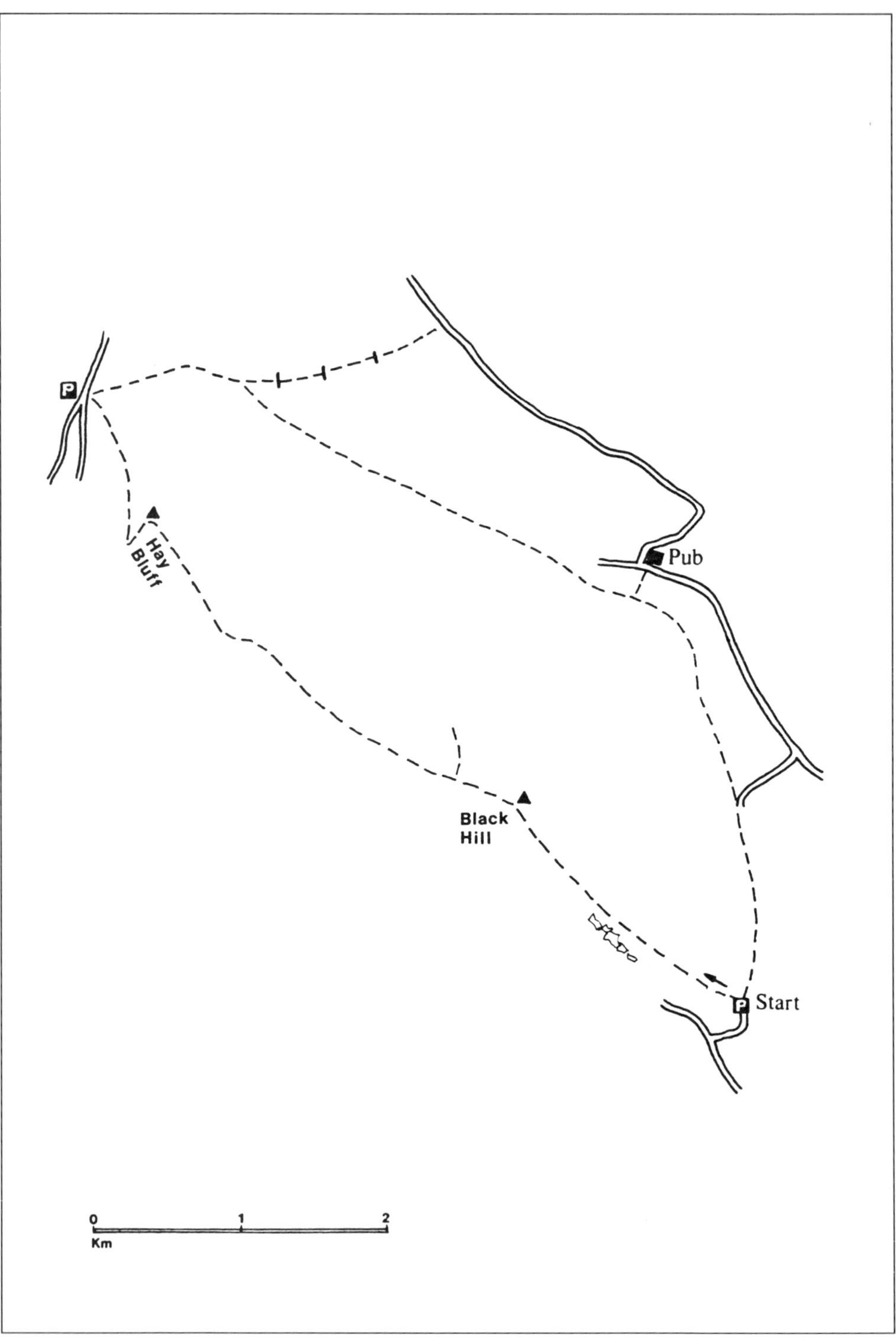
Pub
Hay Bluff
Black Hill
Start
0
1
2
Km

# ROUTE 9

## The Black Hill and the Bull's Head

**Distance:** 15km (9 miles)
**Walking Time There:** 3 hours
**Back:** $1^1/_2$ hours
**Terrain:** Open mountain and road
**Paths:** Distinct and easy to follow

The initial walk to the top of the Black Hill is steep but soon levels out. There are many small tracks that criss-cross the Black Hill, but as long as you stay on the top and walk in a north-westerly direction they will all lead to Hay Bluff. If the wind is right you will often be entertained by people practising paragliding off the top of the ridge. As you descend the northern face of Hay Bluff you can enjoy the extensive views across the Wye valley and westwards to the Brecon Beacons. The pub is called The Bull's Head and is very popular with walkers and equestrians alike. The food is simple but good and there is a range of good ales. Inside the bar is very small and cosy but there is plenty of seating outside in the garden. The carpark at the start of the route can easily be found by taking the road to Longtown from the A465. After Longtown take the road signposted Llanveynoe – the turning to the carpark is signposted about 4km ($2^1/_2$ miles) on the right.

1. Start at the carpark and picnic site at the top of the Olchon valley below the ridge of the Black Hill, SO288329.
2. Leave the carpark and follow the footpath that climbs up the narrow ridge, known as the cat's back, to the trig' point at the top of the Black Hill – approx $2^1/_2$km.
3. From the trig' point take the obvious path to the left towards the summit of Hay Bluff $3^1/_2$km away. In the distance you will see Hay Bluff and to your left is the Hatterall ridge along which the Offa's Dyke footpath runs; you will soon meet this ridge.
4. Follow the footpath below the Hatterall ridge and join the Offa's Dyke footpath at the end. Stay on this path until you reach the trig' point on the top of Hay Bluff.
5. Take the right hand path from the trig' point and follow it down the northern scarp of Hay Bluff.
6. Stay on the track until it meets the road at the bottom, near to the carparking area, and then turn hard right to follow a bridleway. This bridleway is a bit indistinct to start with but soon becomes more obvious.
7. Follow the bridleway through three gates and across a field until you reach a narrow road. Turn right at this road and follow it for $2^1/_2$km to the Bull's Head pub at Craswall.
8. Come out of the pub and turn left onto the road.
9. Walk for 100m and then turn right up a bridleway.

*The Vale of Ewyas from Hay Bluff.*

*The odd shape of the forest below Hay Bluff.*

10. After 250m there is a junction – turn left and follow this bridleway for 1km until it reaches a rough road. Carry straight on in the same direction.
11. The rough road soon reverts to a track and should be followed back to the carpark.

**Alternative Route A:** $7^1/_2$km ($4^1/_2$ miles)

1. Park at the carpark below the Black Hill and walk along the bridleway to the right.
2. The bridleway turns into a rough road which can be followed downhill to a junction – turn left at the junction and follow the road to the pub.
3. Upon leaving the pub follow the return route as above.

**Alternative Route B:** 10km (6 miles)

1. Start at the carpark below Hay Bluff, SO239373, and follow the main route from instruction number 6 to the pub. The track runs to the left of Hay Bluff which rises above the carpark.
2. Upon leaving the pub follow instructions 8 & 9, but at the junction at the top of the bridleway (instruction 10) turn right instead of left and follow the track back to the carpark.

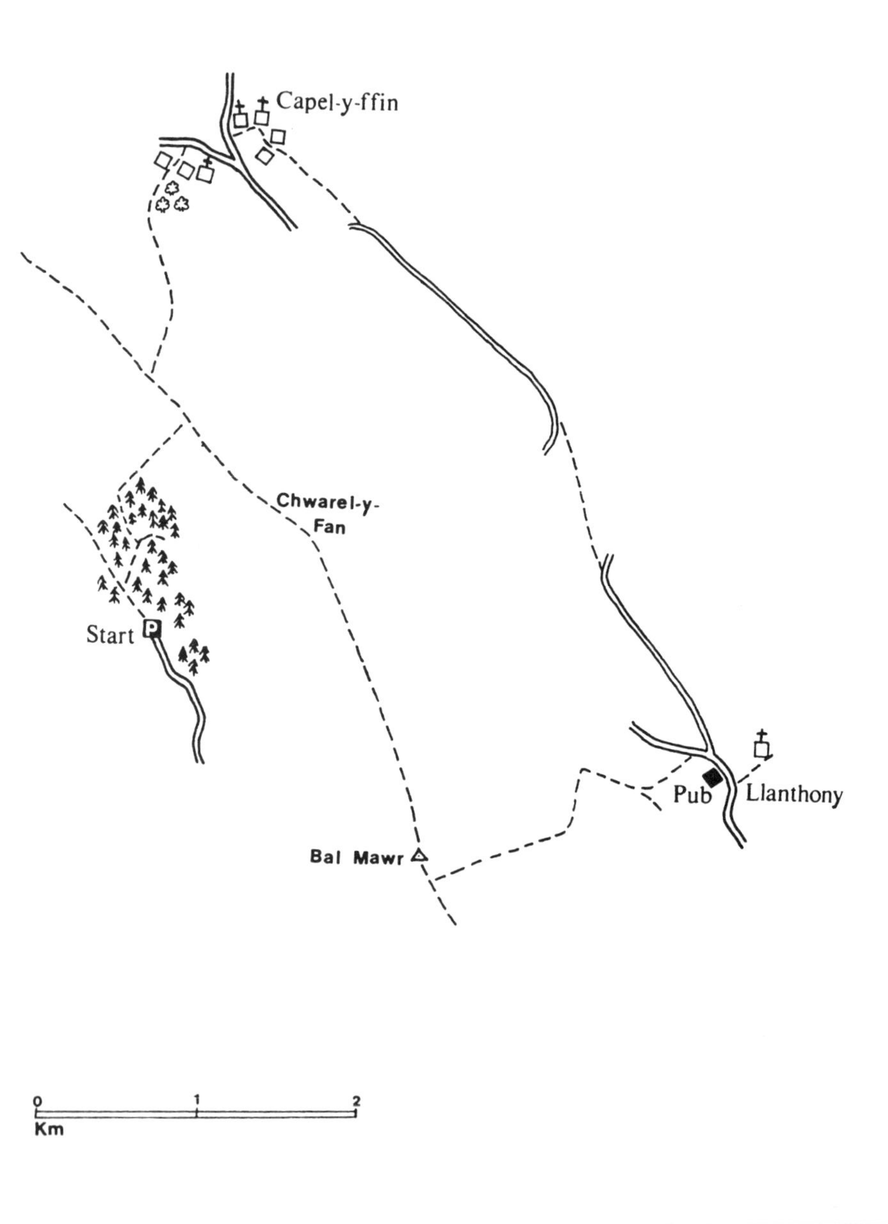
Capel-y-ffin
Chwarel-y-
Fan
Start
Bal Mawr
Pub
Llanthony
0
1
2
Km

# ROUTE 10

## Vale of Ewyas and Llanthony

**Distance:** 15½km (9½ miles)
**Walking Time There:** 2½ hours
**Back:** 2 hours
**Terrain:** Open mountain and trackways, some steep slopes
**Paths:** Clear and well marked

This route takes you over the high ridge of Charwel y Fan and then down into the well known Vale of Ewyas. Near to the pony trekking centre will be seen the ruins of the church that was attached to the now privately owned monastery buildings originally built by Father Ignatius. Further down the road is the small church of St. Mary which is worth a visit. A Baptist chapel is hidden away behind some trees a short distance along the track from St. Mary's. The Half Moon Inn is small with stone floors, a pool table and wood burning stove. It caters for walkers and provides cheap and basic food along with real ale supplied by the Bullmastiff brewery of Penarth in South Glamorgan: their strong ale is called 'Son of a Bitch' which may raise some eyebrows. Nearby are the ruins of Llanthony Priory which was founded in the 12th century by Augustine monks. Part of the priory has now been converted into a hotel at which the bar provides an alternative to the Half Moon Inn. The return walk is back over the ridge and is quite steep to begin with.

1. Start at the carpark at the end of the road in the Grwyne Fawr valley, SO251286.
2. Walk up the track from the carpark with the plantation to your right. Turn right at a sign for Capel y Ffin and follow the horse symbols through the forest to the open mountain.
3. Go through a gate, turn right and walk directly up the slope to the top of the ridge above.
4. Turn left onto a path at the top of the ridge.
5. After 600m you will come to a large cairn. Take the right hand track at the nearby fork.
6. Follow the track down the steep sides of the Vale of Ewyas heading to the left of the trees below. Cross a stream and follow the track to a gate at the rear of the pony trekking centre.
7. Walk through the centre and down to the road beyond. The ruins of the monastery's church can be visited to the right of the pony trekking centre, before walking to the road.
8. Turn right at the road and proceed for 250m. Turn left at a junction and walk along the road into the village of Capel y Ffin.
9. After 100m turn right through a gate and onto the track just before the church of St. Mary. Follow the yellow arrow.
10. Follow this track past the second church on your left. Continue along the track between a house and a barn and then follow the yellow arrows through fields. When the path meets a lane go straight on.

*The church of St. Mary in Capel y Ffin.*

11. When the lane bends sharply to the right just before Trevelog bridge go straight on through a gate and onto a path.
12. This path then meets another lane which can be followed to the Half Moon Inn.
13. Emerge from the pub and turn left along the road and over a bridge. 350m after the bridge turn left and follow a narrow track uphill between trees.
14. After 250m go through a gate onto the open mountain and turn right along a path. Go left at the next path junction and continue up the steep side of the cwm.
15. Come to a path junction 500m beyond the top of the cwm. Turn right and follow the path up the steep ascent to the top of Bal Mawr.
16. Follow the distinct path along the ridge from Bal Mawr to the rocky summit of Chwarel y Fan.
17. Turn left about 500m past the summit and head downhill to the right of the plantation. Retrace your steps through the plantation onto the rough road and back to the carpark.

**Alternative Route:** 10km (6 miles)
This route cuts out the mountain section leaving for easy walking through the countryside of the Vale of Ewyas. Start at Capel y Ffin – join the main route at instruction number 9 to the pub. Return the same way or along the road if the traffic is quiet. This is a good route if you can get someone to drop you off at Capel y Ffin and pick you up from the pub or the nearby Llanthony Priory.

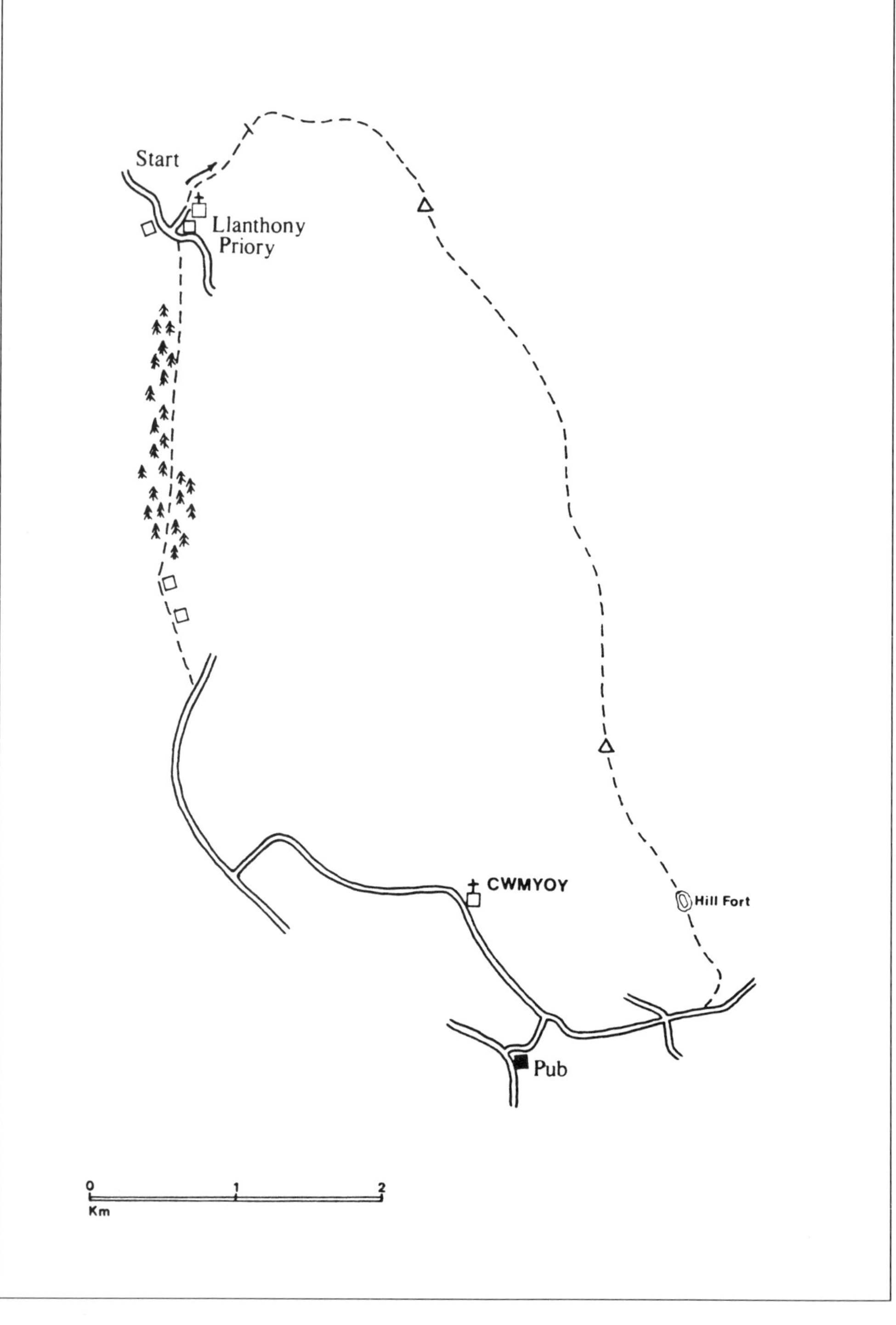
Start
Llanthony
Priory
CWMYOY
Hill Fort
Pub
0
1
2
Km

# ROUTE 11

## Llanthony Priory and The Queens Head

**Distance:** 17km ($10^1/_2$ miles)
**Walking Time There:** 3 hours
**Back:** 2 hours
**Terrain:** Open mountain, valley and forest tracks
**Paths:** Well marked out and easy to follow

This route combines the great openness of the Hatterall ridge with a pleasant walk back in the valley. The ridge catches the wind from the east and is popular with many people for paragliding, handgliding and flying model gliders. On the way down from the ridge you pass through the remains of an Iron Age hillfort; only the banks and ditches of the ramparts now survive. Across the valley to the west can be seen a better example of a hillfort called Twyn y Gaer. It is easy to imagine the problems that attackers would have met when trying to get to the top of the steep rampart circled summit. The pub is called the Queens Head and has a small and cosy bar with a stone floor and large wood burning stove. They serve real ales and a good selection of food, all of which can be enjoyed in the garden. Walkers are welcomed. On the way back it is worthwhile stopping at the church of Cwmyoy. This church was built on unstable ground and has now twisted in a most peculiar fashion – the effect inside is like a fairground funhouse where no two verticals lie in the same plane. The return route takes an easy to follow track along the side of the valley which makes a change from the open mountain.

1. Start at Llanthony Priory carpark, SO289278.
2. Follow the path marked by yellow arrows from the side of the priory opposite the church. Go over the stile next to the gate and turn right onto a track.
3. Follow the track for 100m and turn left across the field to a stile.
4. Cross the stile and walk diagonally up the next field to another stile. Continue across the field heading for the open ground above.
5. Keep following the path uphill across the open mountain towards the top of the ridge.
6. Follow the narrow path around to the right. Walk across the top of the open mountain to your left until you meet the Offa's Dyke footpath that runs across the top. Turn right onto this path and follow it for 5km past one trig' point and on to the next.
7. Continue to follow the Offa's Dyke footpath downhill through a hillfort. Keep to the left of a wall and then over a stile and onto a path bounded by fences on either side. Turn right along the road at the bottom.
8. Walk uphill for 500m – come to a crossroads and go straight across and then down the steep hill beyond.

*The ruins of Llanthony Priory.*

9. After 1km you will meet another road – turn left.
10. Follow this road downhill and then up a slight incline for a short distance to the Queens Head at the top.
11. From the pub turn right and back down the road that you came on.
12. Walk along this country lane for 2km into the village of Cwmyoy and stop to see the odd church.
13. After the church continue along the country lane, cross the river Honddu and join the road. Turn right at this road.
14. Walk along the road for 1km and turn left up a track marked with a public footpath sign.
15. At the top of the track go over a stile next to a gate just before the cottage. Go to the right and walk up to the forest track above the cottage.
16. Follow this track through the forest and join the main forest track above a farmhouse – the route along here is well marked.
17. Walk along the forest track for 2km until you come to a stile marked with a yellow arrow on the right. Go over the stile and follow the narrow path across the field to another stile.
18. Walk diagonally across the next two fields – cross the stream at the bottom and then keep to the left.
19. Cross the river via the narrow footbridge and follow the track opposite to the road. Turn left at the road and then immediately right up the access road of the priory and back to the carpark.

**Alternative Route:** 6km ($3^1/_2$ miles)
Start at Llanthony Priory and follow the route to instruction 6 but stop at the first trig' point. There are excellent views from across the top of this ridge and it is worth the climb up. Return via the same route. Refreshments can be sought before you walk or when you return from either the hotel bar at the priory or from the Half Moon Inn a little way along the main road. (see route 10 for the Half Moon Inn).

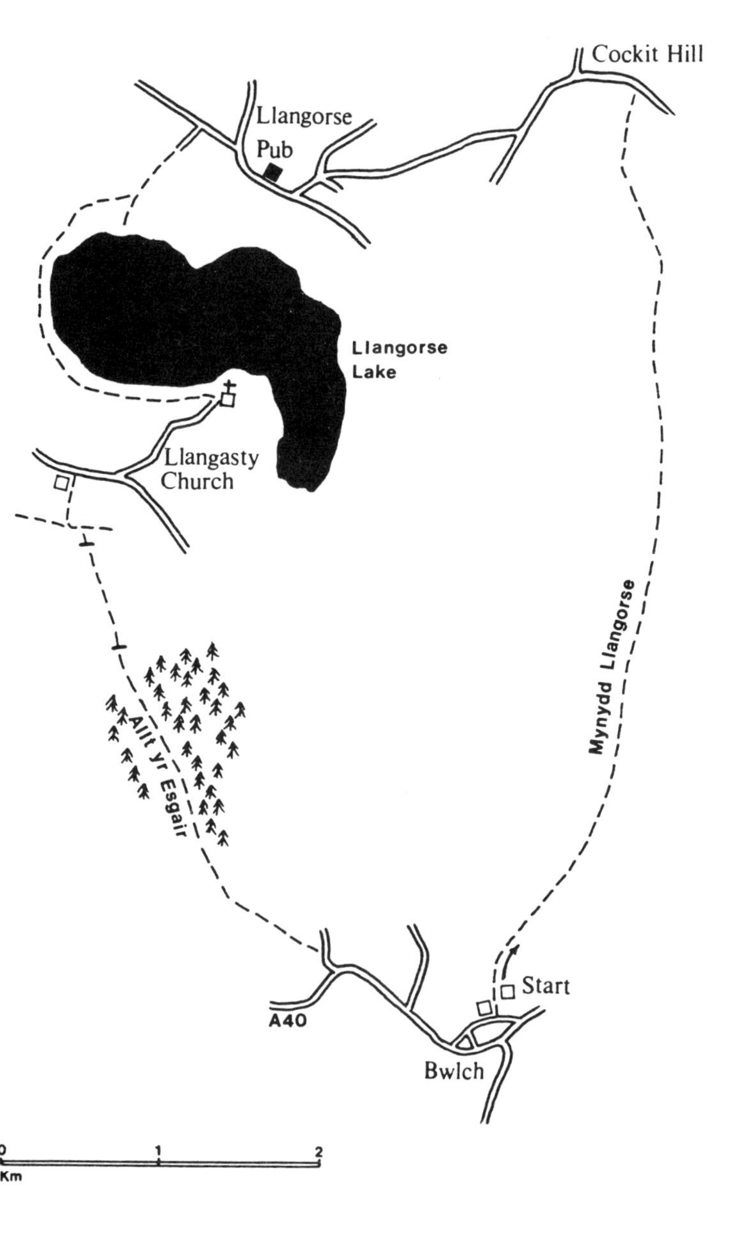
Cockit Hill
Llangorse
Pub
Llangorse
Lake
Llangasty
Church
Allt yr Esgair
Mynydd Llangorse
Start
A40
Bwlch
0
1
2
Km

# ROUTE 12

## Mountain and Lake of Llangorse

**Distance:** 18km (11 miles)
**Walking Time There:** 2½ hours
**Back:** 2½ hours
**Terrain:** Generally easy going
**Paths:** Clear and easy to follow

The long walk across the top of Mynydd Llangorse starts with a gentle uphill gradient and then drops down quite steeply at the end. Fine views can be had across the Usk valley to the right and the area around Llangorse Lake to the left. The Castle Inn at Llangorse is a traditional style pub with bar games and no electronic machines making irritating noises. The bar has a stone floor and the proprietors are welcoming to the weary walker. Good food is on offer as well as draught beer and both are served in a warm and friendly atmosphere. It is recommended in the 1991 Good Beer Guide. There is a pleasant walk around the lake, but the edges are overgrown with reeds and the path can become boggy in wet weather. The church of Llangasty-Talyllyn is beautifully situated and is a good place to view the lake. The walk along the ridge of Allt yr Esgair is far better than returning along the road and provides extensive views across the Brecon Beacons. Below the ridge is the Usk valley and the village of Talybont.

1. Start at the village of Bwlch on the A40, SO150220.
2. Walk up the lane to the left of the post office in Bwlch. After a short distance meet another road and turn right.
3. Turn left onto a bridleway shortly after passing a large white house. This bridleway is very clear and should be followed up and across the top of Mynydd Llangorse.
4. After walking for 6km the bridleway drops down into the gap between Mynydd Troed and Mynydd Llangorse, called Cockit Hill. Here find a road and turn left along it.
5. After 500m turn left at a junction.
6. After another 500m turn right and follow the road into the village of Llangorse where you will find the Castle Inn on the right.
7. Upon leaving the pub turn right and then follow the signs for Llangorse Lake which will take you down a narrow road.
8. When you reach the information and map board at the bottom of the road turn right, cross the field and head for a narrow footbridge.
9. Cross this footbridge and follow the yellow arrows. Go diagonally across the first field to a stile and then again to steps over a wall.
10. After the steps go diagonally across the field to the opposite corner and another stile. After this the path becomes more obvious to the church of Llangasty-Talyllyn.

*The church of Llangasty-Talyllyn.*

*Llangorse Lake from Mynydd Llangorse.*

11. The path joins the road near the church of Llangasty-Talyllyn. Turn right and follow the road away from the church and lake.
12. After 800m you will come to a junction – turn right in the direction of Pennorth. (At this point you could turn left and follow the road back to Bwlch).
13. Walk for 400m along the road until you come to a hall. Turn left onto a track just before the hall.
14. After 300m the track meets another – turn left and walk for 100m to a metal gate – do not go through this gate but turn right and go through a small wooden gate and follow the track uphill to the top of Allt y Esgair.
15. Follow the track down the opposite side. About halfway down you will meet a gap in the wall in front of you that is blocked by an old fence – go through or over this and continue downhill to a gate and a lane.
16. Go straight on when the lane meets a road. After 200m this road takes you back to the A40, onto which you should turn left and follow for about 500m back to the village of Bwlch.

**Alternative Route:** 7km (4½ miles)
Park at the end of the road near the lake and Llangasty church, SO133261. Go over the stile at the side of the carpark and follow the yellow arrows around the outside of the lake to the footbridge near the sailing club buildings. Turn left along the track away from the lake and sailing club. Turn right at the top of this track and follow the road into Llangorse. Return by the same route from instruction number 7 – unfortunately there is no footpath around the other side of the lake.

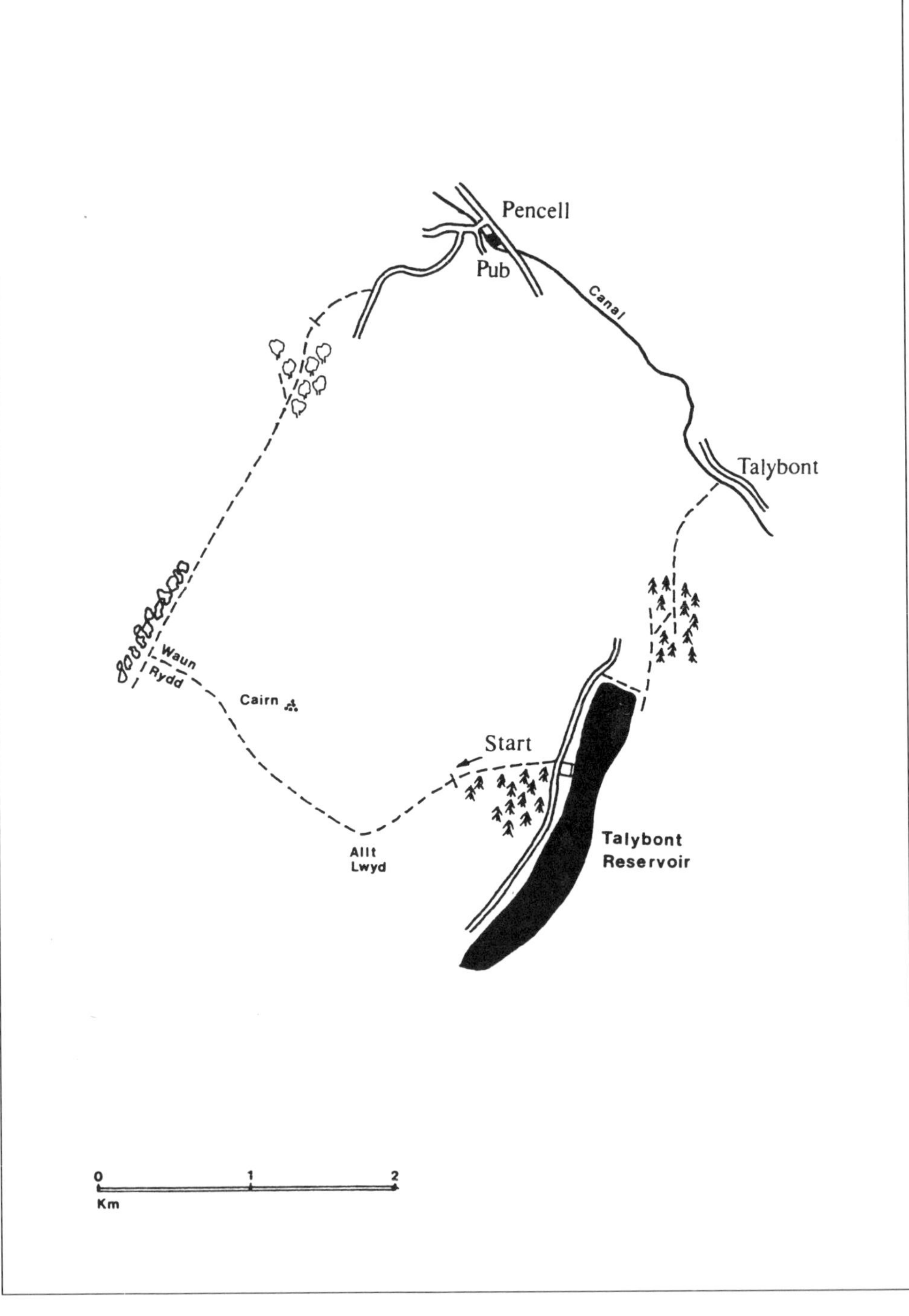
Pencell
Pub
Canal
Talybont
Waun
Rydd
Cairn
Start
Allt
Lwyd
Talybont
Reservoir
0
1
2
Km

# ROUTE 13

## Waun Rydd and Canal Towpath

**Distance:** 19km (12 miles)
**Walking Time There:** $3^1/_4$ hours
**Back:** $1^1/_2$ hours
**Terrain:** Open mountain followed by canal towpath
**Paths:** Reasonable on the mountain and very good elsewhere

This walk may seem long but it is only the initial steep ascent to Waun Rydd that can be considered difficult; after that the route becomes quite easy and the section along the canal after the pub can be considered leisurely. There are extensive views across the wide glacial valleys of the Beacons from Allt Lwyd and Waun Rydd. From the western ridge of Waun Rydd the whole of the Brecon Beacons range spreads out, rising to the highest peaks in the park – Pen y Fan and Corn Du. The Royal Oak at Pencelli is used to walkers as there is a camp site nearby. It has stone and tile floors and serves the usual bar foods. The range of beers is not great but this is countered by the garden which is set in a perfect position alongside the canal. The canal towpath makes a pleasant walk and can be followed all the way to Talybont-on-Usk. It is possible to stop at one of the pubs in Talybont, instead of, or as well as, the one in Pencelli. After Talybont the route continues along an easy to walk track and finishes by crossing the dam and following the edge of the huge Talybont reservoir.

1. Start at the parking area that overlooks the Talybont reservoir, about 1km SW of the dam, SO099196.
2. Walk up the Forestry Commission track and bridleway on the opposite side of the road from the carpark. After 100m a blue arrow directs you over a stile and up the hill.
3. Continue to follow the narrow paths uphill with the forest to your left. Go through a gate at the top of the field that gives access to the open mountain.
4. After going through the gate you will see in front of you a large curved ridge – walk straight up the steep slope to your front which leads to the left end of the ridge; this hill is called Allt Lwyd.
5. Go over the top of Allt Lwyd and continue along the ridge via a narrow path. Follow this path up the steep slope to Waun Rydd.
6. Follow a narrow path NW across the gently undulating summit of Waun Rydd, passing a small cairn on the way. Walk towards the peaks of Pen y Fan and Corn Du that can be seen in the distance.
7. After crossing Waun Rydd you will come to the edge of the ridge from which the rest of the Beacons can be seen. Turn right at this ridge to follow another small path.

*The Talybont reservoir.*

8. After approx 3km the path drops down towards the farmland. Follow the path around to the right until you meet a stile next to a gate. Continue along the track after the gate.
9. After 600m the track meets a narrow lane – turn left. The village of Pencelli can be seen below.
10. Follow the lane downhill to meet a road – turn right. On the way you will see Llanfeigan Church nestling amongst trees on the other side of a stream.
11. After a short distance the canal will be met. Cross the canal via a bridge. Shortly after meet a road and turn right into the village of Pencelli where you will find The Royal Oak.
12. The canal towpath can now be reached from the garden at the rear of the pub – turn left onto the towpath.
13. Continue along the towpath for 3km until you come to a white drawbridge and the village of Talybont-on-Usk.
14. Walk along the towpath above the village and cross the bridge over the canal at the rear of the White Hart Inn.
15. Follow the track beyond the bridge. After a short distance go over a bridge that crosses the deep cutting of a dismantled railway and continue to follow the track.
16. Go through a wooden gate surrounded by forest and shortly after turn right down a forestry road to join another track – turn left at this track and follow it to the reservoir dam.
17. Walk across the top of the dam and turn left at the road. The carpark is on the left 1km along this road.

**Alternative Route A:** 6km (4 miles)
Start at either the village of Pencelli or Talybont and walk along the canal towpath that joins them. Return by the same route. (For the pubs available in Talybont see route 5).

**Alternative Route B:** 8km (5 miles)
Start at the same carpark as the main route. Instead of walking up to the mountains follow the route back across the reservoir dam and along the track to the village of Talybont, returning the same way.

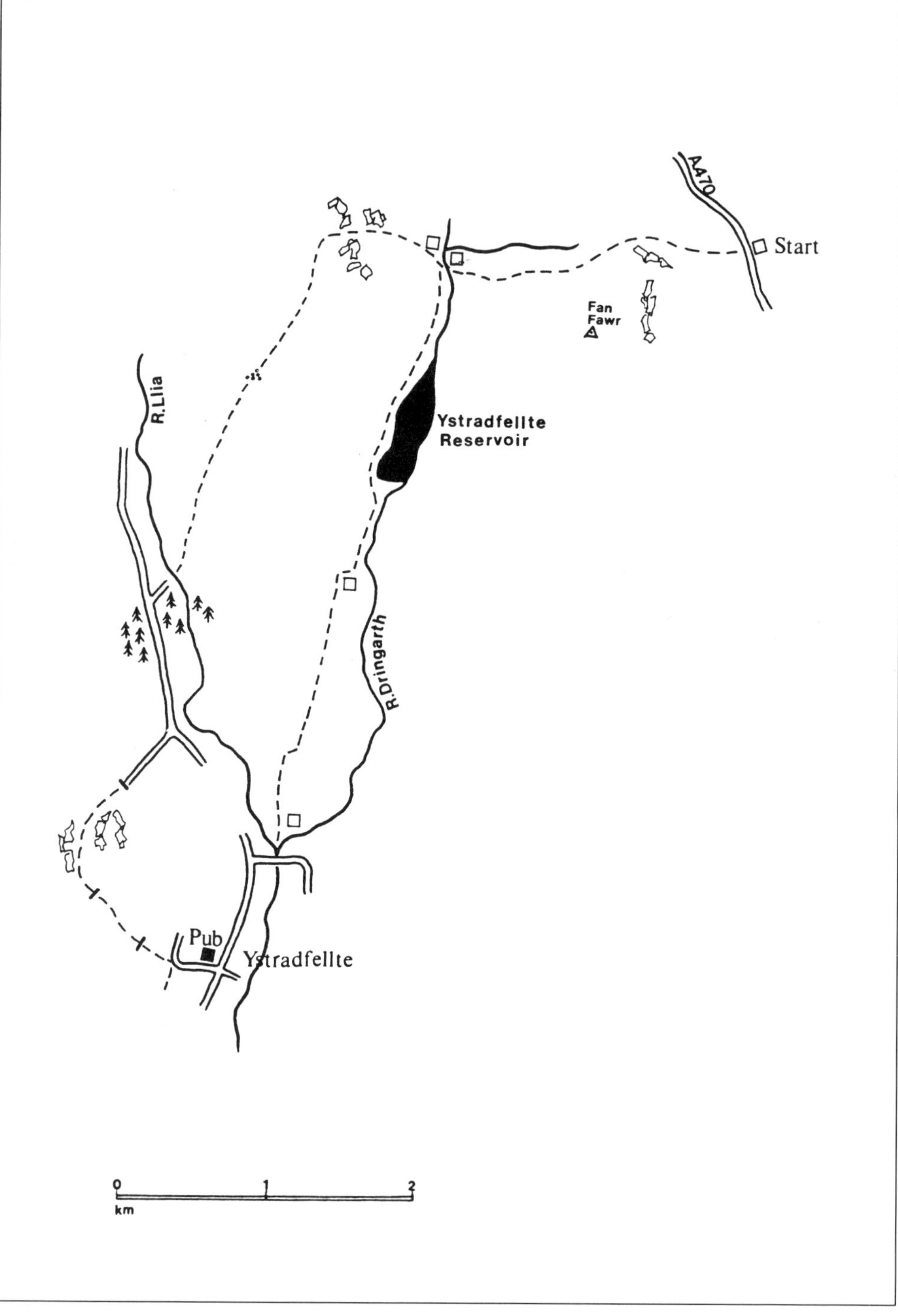
A470
Start
Fan
Fawr
R.Llia
Ystradfellte
Reservoir
R.Dringarth
Pub
Ystradfellte
0
1
2
km

# ROUTE 14

## Fan Dringarth and Ystradfellte

**Distance:** 21km (13 miles)
**Walking Time There:** 3½ hours
**Back:** 3 hours
**Terrain:** Very rough open mountain with steep ascents and descents
**Paths:** Few on the mountains, map & compass recommended

This is a very arduous walk that will take all day and should not be attempted in bad weather. The first 2km around the base of Fan Fawr can often be very boggy and wet. There is a hard climb to the top of Fan Dringarth but it is worth the effort as the views are spectacular. The New Inn in Ystradfellte is pleasant and is often frequented by caving groups exploring the nearby cave systems: it serves Whitbread beer and good bar food. The route back from the pub cuts through farmland before following the river Mellte and the Ystradfellte reservoir up the valley – there is no real footpath here just sheep tracks which can be difficult but it makes a nice change to get close to the noisy river and then the tranquil waters of the reservoir.

1. Start at the carpark opposite Storey Arms on the A470, SN982203.
2. Go over one of the stiles from the carpark and walk west. A narrow path can be followed around the northern slopes of Fan Fawr. Keep the steep slopes of Fan Fawr to your left.
3. Continue walking west for 2km. In front you will see Fan Dringarth – it is this mountain that you are heading for. Drop down into the valley of the Ystradfellte reservoir and cross the river Dringarth near the ruins of a farmhouse and sheep-pens.
4. Continue in a westerly direction up the steep side of the valley to the summit of Fan Dringarth.
5. When you reach the top turn left and follow a narrow path SW across to the summit of Fan Llia where you will find a cairn.
6. Continue walking SW into the valley of the Afon Llia which is to the right. Head for the forestry plantation that can be seen in the distance. Walk towards where the narrow road below enters the forestry plantation. Nearby will be seen some sheepfolds and a picnic area. Two stiles near the river will allow you access to the picnic area where you can cross the river via a small weir.
7. Walk up the track from the picnic area and turn left onto the road which should be followed for 800m.
8. Turn onto a track that will be directly ahead of you as the road takes a sharp left hand bend. Follow the track between limestone walls for about 1km until a gate to the rocky area is reached.
9. Go through the gate – immediately the track forks, take the left hand side and follow the track between the limestone crags of Carnau Gwynion. Go through another gate and keep to the left as the track becomes less obvious.

*The rough limestone of Carnau Gwynion.*

10. Go through another gate and onto a grassy track. Follow the track onto a rough road and continue downhill to the pub at Ystradfellte.
11. Leave the pub and turn left. Walk along the road for 1km and turn right. After 200m go across the bridge over the river Llia and turn left onto a track marked with a bridleway sign.
12. Follow the bridleway markers past a farm and along the track to a gate. Turn right at the gate and walk for a short distance to a stile. The field beyond this stile is large and should be crossed diagonally to another gate – follow the posts that have been erected to guide you.
13. Continue along the bridleway, past a ruined farmhouse, and down to meet the river Dringarth. Turn left at the river and follow it upstream to the reservoir.
14. Walk around the edge of the reservoir and continue to follow the river Dringarth upstream.
15. When you reach the ruined farmhouse that you past on the outward journey cross the river and head back along the same route. To your left will be a stream known as Nant Mawr running in a distinctive wide cutting. Keep Nant Mawr to your left. When you reach the flat ground you will see the peak of Corn Du in the distance – walk towards this peak until you can see Storey Arms and the carpark below.

**Alternative Route:** 7km (4 miles)

1. Start at the carpark and picnic area at SN928165 and follow the main route from instruction number 7 to the pub.
2. After leaving the pub turn right and retrace your steps back to the carpark.